SAM ADAMS
The Boy Who Became
Father of the American Revolution

Sam Adams

5.95
4.46

SAM ADAMS
The Boy Who Became
Father of the American Revolution

by Fayette Richardson
illustrated by William Sauts Bock

CROWN PUBLISHERS, INC., NEW YORK

Library of Congress Cataloging in Publication Data

Richardson, Fayette, 1923–
    Sam Adams; the boy who became father of the American Revolution.

    SUMMARY: A brief biography of the Massachusetts radical whose belief in forceful protest against injustice made him one of the leaders of the Revolution.
    1. Adams, Samuel, 1722–1803—Juvenile literature.
[1. Adams, Samuel, 1722–1803. 2. United States—History—Revolution, 1775–1803—Biography] I. Bock, William Sauts, 1939–   illus. II. Title.
E302.6.A2R52   1975   973.3'092'4 [B]
  [92] 74-83211
ISBN 0-517-51847-3

From a place on top of the Adams house in Boston Sam could watch ships sailing out at sea.

Sometimes his father would say, "Let's go down to the dock, Sam." He'd take Sam's hand and they'd go down to the Adams dock where men were unloading a big ship. The men would carry out bundles and boxes from inside the ship. Sam's father was a merchant who bought these things and then sold them to other people.

But Sam was more interested in the men who unloaded the ships, the "mechanicks." Any man who did hard work like that was a mechanick. They'd wave to him and talk to him and give him rides.

"Climb on my back, Sam," a friend named Bill said.

Bill's back was hard and strong. He carried Sam down into the ship.

"What makes that smell, Bill?" Sam asked.

"Lots of things," said Bill. "Things like spices and tea and old wood and salt water and stuff like that."

"What's that noise?" asked Sam.

"Just the timbers stretching a little after the long voyage from England," Bill said.

"Where is that?"

"Clear across the ocean—where King George sits on a throne."

"Does he really sit on a throne, Bill?"

"Sure and he eats roast beef and gravy and I have to work hard all day and go home and eat corn bread."

That did not seem fair.

When Sam was back on the dock his father was waiting for him.

"What does the king do?" Sam asked him.

"He rules England and America."

"He makes laws for you and me?"

"Well," said his father, frowning a little, "it's like this. We vote for men in the town house to make our laws and . . ."

"The king doesn't make our laws?"

"Well, he picks the governor who sits in our town house, the governor for our colony of Massachusetts Bay."

Sam had seen the town house. It was a big brick building with gold statues on the roof. On one side of the roof there was a lion standing on his hind feet and on the other side was a unicorn, an animal with a long horn in the middle of his forehead.

"And," his father went on, "the king meets with Parliament. That's a group of men in England who make laws for everybody."

"But not for us."

His father frowned. "Yes, they can make laws for us too."

"But you said that men here made our laws," Sam said.

"They do!" said his father.

"But the king and Parliament can make laws for us too!" said Sam.

"That's true," agreed his father, "but when our Puritan forefathers came here they settled in the wilderness and they made all their own laws. Every man in the church could vote in those days. Then it was changed."

His father told him about the first Puritans who had sailed across the sea to escape unfair laws and had built their houses in the dark cold woods of Massachusetts. Sam listened and tried to picture them.

"Weren't they afraid?" he said.

"Sometimes," said his father. "Everybody is afraid sometimes. But they were brave and they wanted to be free to make their own laws."

They were walking from the dock toward the tall white Adams house. A farmer driving a wagon came toward them. The wagon was full of apples.

"I'd like to buy some of the cloth I hear you're unloading, Mr. Adams. Could you take some apples for it?"

"I already have a cellar full of apples," said Sam's father.

"I need some cloth," said the farmer.

Sam turned to his father, "Could he sell them for silver and then give you silver for your cloth?"

"Trouble is," said the farmer, "no one has much gold or silver. People want to trade me things like corn and I got plenty of corn. How about some bills of credit, Mr. Adams? I know they ain't worth much but they're better than nothing."

Sam's father and the farmer went on trying to figure out a way to trade. Sam's father finally took the bills of credit.

Hard money (gold and silver) was scarce in Massachusetts. Most people had to spend what they had to buy high-priced British goods that weren't made or grown in the colony. Things like iron tools, paper, cloth, or tea. Because prices were high, hard money had a way of getting back to Britain—or ending up in the strongboxes of the wealthiest Boston merchants, who were friends of Britain and who ran the colony. These men got things done the way they wanted by asking favors of their friend the governor. He gave them good jobs in the government where they could decide things. They also gave presents or good jobs to men who

were supposed to be representatives of the people. Then these representatives would vote the way the wealthy merchants wanted.

Sam's father was a merchant too. But he was not part of the group that ran the town. He did not like what they did. He was part of a group who was against them.

Sam had started going to grammar school when the new governor arrived. His name was Governor Belcher and Sam's father said that he had an order from the king to stop the colony from using bills of credit, and that was bad.

"Why is it bad?" asked Sam.

"People don't have gold and silver to pay the high prices and if we don't have some other money we won't be able to buy and sell."

"Then the king shouldn't do that," Sam said.

Sam had to get up in the dark to walk to the town house to go to school. Mister Lovell taught him and the other boys (girls went to a different school) arithmetic and reading and Latin. At noon Sam ran all the way home to eat lunch. He was good in his studies and he was the leader of the other boys in planning games and going on hikes.

But one day, after Mr. Lovell had told them about the Puritans again, Sam did not go out to play. He started writing. He

wrote a story about "liberty." He said people should have liberty to talk over things and decide what laws should be made. Like the founding fathers. He said everybody should be ready to fight for liberty. He said liberty was more important than money. It was more important than nice clothes. It was more important than good things to eat.

He brought the paper home to his father. His father read it and looked at it for a long time before he said anything. Then he looked at Sam.

"That's good, Sam. It's very good." That was all his father said. He didn't smile; he just nodded his head and looked at Sam and nodded his head some more.

Sam was proud.

That night he lay awake in his bed for a long time thinking about how he would fight for liberty when he was big.

Days at school were very long—from early morning until evening. But Sam worked hard, and when he was only fourteen he passed tests to go to Harvard College. Harvard was in a little town outside Boston and he had to go there and live in a building with other students. On holidays he came home.

One day when Sam went home he heard his father talking with some other men in the living room. They were excited.

After the meeting was over, his father said, "Sam, boy, we're going to make our own money. We've begun what we call a 'land bank.' We'll print money and we've pledged our land and homes so that the money will be good."

Wealthy merchants like Mr. Thomas Hutchinson did not like the land bank.

"It's a wicked plan," Hutchinson announced to men in the town house where he was a representative.

"I don't know," said another man. "The land bankers say it'll help our money problem."

"It won't work!" shouted Hutchinson. "Most of them have hardly a penny to their name—all except for Adams."

To wealthy merchants like himself Hutchinson whispered, "It's a very wicked scheme. If it works people won't need our English money so bad and that means it won't be worth so much. We'll have to pay more when we buy people's corn or fish or apples or they'll take it to someone who'll pay them in land bank money!"

"We'll lose money!" said another merchant.

"That's not all we'll lose," warned Hutchinson. "We'll lose some of our power to run this town. If the land bank works people won't feel they have to listen to us—they'll listen to Adams and his kind."

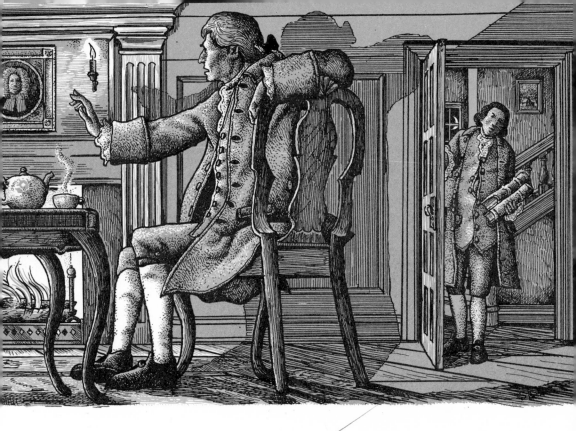

In the newspapers Hutchinson's friends wrote angry articles saying the land bankers were dishonest and out to cheat people.

In spite of this, most people thought the land bank was a good idea. And they offered to trade with land bank bills.

So Hutchinson and his friends decided on another way to stop the land bank. They wrote their friends in Parliament and soon Parliament passed a law that said the land bank must stop printing money.

Sam was home from school when this happened and he listened as land bank men met in the Adams's living room and talked angrily about the law.

"Parliament has no right to do this!" shouted one.

"We should get guns," said another. "It's time to fight." Yes, Sam thought. It was wrong and they should act.

When Sam's father sat down at the supper table that night his face was sad. He shook his head slowly.

"The land bank is finished," he said. "I don't know what we'll do."

"But they have no right to do that!" Sam cried. "The colony needs it. The people want it. Parliament cannot take away the people's rights! We should fight!"

"We're not ready to fight," said his father sadly. "And now they even want to take our land and homes because we pledged them to the land bank."

Sam did not forget about Parliament or the land bank. When he graduated from Harvard he made a speech that said people of Massachusetts should not obey a law passed by the king's government if that law took away the right of the colony to rule itself.

The people of Boston showed they liked Sam's father and what he had done by electing him to be their representative in the town house—and by voting out Thomas Hutchinson. A new governor, Governor William Shirley, said that Sam's father and the other land bank men would have to pay large sums of money or lose their land and homes.

"But," said Sam's father, "we did not close the bank. An unfair law did."

"Nevertheless, you must pay," the governor said.

Then something changed the governor's mind. A war began between the English and the French. Governor Shirley needed the help of everyone. "I've decided we can settle this in a friendly way," he said, and he stopped saying he would take away the land bank men's homes and property.

Sam's father worked hard in the Massachusetts government

during the war. When the war was over he became sick and died. Sam was now the master of the Adams household.

He began a newspaper and spoke against wealthy families like the Hutchinsons who ran the Massachusetts government. Thomas

Hutchinson and others had regained important jobs. Sam said these men talked of "liberty" but their actions showed that the only liberty they cared about was their own freedom to bully and cheat poorer and weaker people.

Many people liked what Sam wrote, but the governor and his friend Mr. Hutchinson did not. Perhaps this was why there were demands again that the land bank men pay large sums of money or lose their homes. A list of debtors was put in the paper. The Adams name topped the list.

Sam did not have much money. And he did not believe the law was fair. He did not pay.

One day the sheriff came to Sam Adams's gate. "I'm here to take your house and sell it," he said.

"You can't take my house!" said Sam.

"Yes, I can. It must be sold to pay the money your father owed for the land bank," said the sheriff.

"My father already paid."

"There is more that must be paid and since you have not paid it I must take your house. That's the law."

"Then the law is wrong. You have no right to take a man's house," Sam said.

"Step aside, Adams," the sheriff said. "These men want to look at the house and may buy it."

Sam's face hardened. "Get off my land!" he shouted.

"Adams, as sheriff I am ordering you to step aside."

"You may be the sheriff," said Sam, "but you are also a citizen of this town and I will sue you for damages if you try to take my house."

As Sam talked, some of his neighbors came and stood behind him scowling at the sheriff. The sheriff began to back up. Then he turned and hurried to his carriage and rode away with the men who had come with him.

Sam had to stop publishing the newspaper. He did not have enough money.

The question now was what kind of work would he do.

His mother had wanted him to be a minister. He did not want to do that. His father had wanted him to be a lawyer. He did not want to do that. He was not happy being a merchant like his father. He did not like buying and selling things. He was always thinking of how to bring back the old puritan spirit of self-government and fair play to the town. He believed that people should govern themselves.

"Things should not be run by a few rich men," he would explain to mechanicks as he sat with them eating lunch on the dock. "Things should be decided by all the people."

He talked to the people of Boston. He kept trying to persuade them they could rule themselves. "You know what the colony needs," he said, "and you can make the laws better than anyone else." He spoke at town meetings. He talked to mechanicks on the docks. He talked to people in stores and taverns and in the streets. He talked to blacksmiths and fishermen. He talked to lawyers and merchants. He talked to farmers who brought their wagons to town.

They listened and they liked what he said. He was elected a representative in the town house. He became the leader of Boston.

One day a ship docked in Boston with bad news. Parliament had passed a law called the Stamp Act. It was a tax. If you lived in America you had to pay a tax if you printed a paper or bought

a house. Even if you bought a deck of cards you had to pay a tax. Times were hard and the people did not have much money.

Also, the law had not been voted on by the people of America or their representatives. The law had been passed by Parliament where they had no voice or vote.

People were angry.

"It's not right," they said. "Other people cannot make laws for us."

Sam Adams brought the people together in a club called the Sons of Liberty. Sometimes people called them Liberty Boys. They were men like silversmith Paul Revere or shoemaker Ebenezer Mackintosh or young schoolboys like eleven-year-old Christopher Snyder, the son of a mechanick.

The Sons of Liberty marched in the streets with signs and

shouted "No stamps!" They said they would not buy any stamps
and they told other people not to buy stamps.

Thomas Hutchinson was now lieutenant governor—as well as
the chief justice. A relative of his, Andrew Oliver, was to be the
stamp seller. The Liberty Boys called on Mr. Oliver. They
knocked on his door and asked him to come to a big meeting
under a big tree they had named the Liberty Tree.

Andrew Oliver was nervous. He was in the middle of thousands of people who said they did not like what he was doing. He said he would not sell any stamps. He would quit being the stamp seller. Everyone cheered.

No one sold stamps. No one bought stamps.

Finally Parliament decided it was no use. Another ship came with news that the Stamp Act was ended.

The Sons of Liberty cheered and had a big celebration. A rich young merchant named John Hancock whom Sam Adams had won to the side of the Liberty Boys gave a big party at his mansion. Bright lanterns were hung in the middle of town and fireworks were fired from ships in the harbor. They lighted up the night sky. Bells rang. Cannons boomed.

But Sam Adams warned, "This is not the end. There will be more bad laws. We must be prepared."

And Sam was right. Soon another law was passed by Parliament that again taxed the people without their having any voice in the matter. This tax was on glass, paint, paper, and tea brought in from Britain.

Sam Adams and the Sons of Liberty said, "Don't buy or sell British goods until they end this law."

Women said, "We like our tea and our tea parties but we won't drink British tea until this tax is stopped. We'll make tea out of herbs from our gardens."

Most merchants agreed to stop selling tea.

But a few would not listen to the Sons of Liberty. They put out tea for sale in their stores.

The Liberty Boys said, "Don't buy from merchants who sell tea."

Then it happened. One cold winter day Christopher Snyder and some other young Liberty Boys put signs in front of the store of a merchant who had tea for sale. One sign was a hand pointing toward the merchant's door. It said, "Don't buy here." Another sign had funny pictures of four merchants who had broken the agreement to sell no tea. It said: "Four fools who love tea better than their town."

A British informer named Richardson came by. He saw the signs and tried to get a farmer to drive his wagon into them and knock them down. The farmer said no. Then several boys saw Richardson and shouted at him. Soon a crowd of boys and others from the town were following the British informer toward his house, shouting at him.

They were very angry. They were doing without things to try to end the unfair tax. He was making it harder for them.

Richardson went into his house and as people gathered outside he brought a gun to the window and fired.

Two boys fell. One of them was Christopher Snyder. When the other boys reached Christopher he was dead.

"All people who love liberty will march in Christopher Snyder's funeral," said Sam Adams.

Thousands marched as Christopher's coffin was carried from the Liberty Tree to the town house and then through the cold snowy streets to the cemetery.

As people stood around the grave, Sam Adams said, "Christopher was only a boy but he loved liberty. And he died for it. We'll never forget him and we'll never buy tea until the tax is ended." X

England had already sent thousands of soldiers to try to frighten the people of Boston. One night there was trouble. Many soldiers were in the streets. Some had brought clubs and swords. They were angry. A few days before there had been a fight between a group of soldiers and some mechanicks who made ropes for ships. The soldiers had been beaten and they had said they would get even. They pushed people and waved their swords and shouted, "Where are your Liberty Boys now? The cowards!"

Near the town house a barber's boy saw a British officer. "Why don't you pay your bill to my master?" he asked.

A soldier standing guard with his musket rushed over to the boy and said, "Show your face!"

"I'll show my face to anyone," the boy said, and as he turned to face the soldier, the soldier hit him with the butt of his musket.

An angry crowd gathered. Other soldiers were soon brought with guns. More people came and shouted at them. Some threw snowballs.

Suddenly an order was given to fire and the soldiers began
shooting.

They killed five men and wounded many more.

The next day people from the town and the country around Boston crowded into Faneuil Hall. Some brought guns. They were determined that the troops must go. Sam Adams spoke to them and then led a small group to the governor's office.

Thomas Hutchinson was now governor.

Hutchinson sat at the council table with the councilmen and the commander of the troops. Above him were pictures of kings in color.

The two men looked at each other for several moments. Sam Adams said, "You must send the troops away."

The governor was worried because he had seen how angry the people were.

"I will send *some* of them away," he said.

"No," Sam Adams said in a hard voice, "You must send *all* of them away."

The governor looked at him. He did not want to send all the troops away because he still hoped to force the people to pay the taxes by using the troops.

Sam Adams pointed his finger at the governor and said, "You must send them all away or what happens will be your doing."

Hutchinson was frightened. He was quiet for a long time and then he said in a low voice, "All right, Adams, I'll send them away."

The soldiers were marched out of the town while people lined the streets and watched. Then it was peaceful. Once again they could walk their streets without trouble.

But the British still refused to end the tax on tea. They decided to lower the tax on tea so that it would be very small—so small that they were sure people would not mind paying it and would once again buy tea.

Sam Adams knew that once the people paid a small tax it would not be the end. It would mean that forever after this the British could tax the people of America and that the tax could get bigger and bigger without their having any voice in the matter.

Ships loaded with tea were sent to Boston and guarded by warships. The British said they were going to land the tea. The Liberty Boys said they were not.

In the back room of the *Boston Gazette*, the Liberty Boys' newspaper, Sam Adams and others met and planned what they would do.

But this time Sam Adams had begun what was really the start of self-government for all America. He had formed the first Committee of Correspondence, which would reach out to all the colonies. This group would work together against unfair British laws. Each town formed a committee of a few men who wrote to other towns and sent their letters by fast horseback riders or ships. Before this, each town felt alone. Now the towns knew what was happening. They knew what the others were doing.

Now all of America was watching and waiting to see what would happen in Boston.

Sam Adams demanded that the tea ships be sent back to Britain. Governor Hutchinson would not give permission for them to leave.

Thousands of people gathered at Old South Church. It was the biggest meeting Boston had ever seen. Many stood outside even though it was December, for there was no more room inside the big church.

A final message was sent to the governor asking him to permit the ships to leave. Then they waited.

Some said they should be careful and not do anything rash. Sam Adams said they must never allow the tea to be landed. Hutchinson did not want to get the message so he went to his country home. But the messengers followed him, and the crowd waited. Sunset came. It became dark. Candles had to be lighted. A final vote was taken on whether they should allow the tea to be landed.

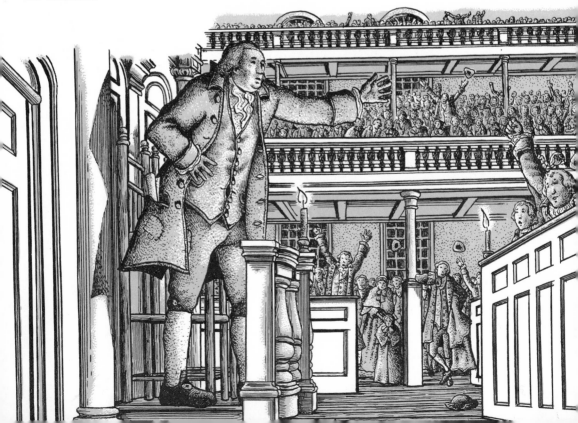

Seven thousand people voted no.

Finally the governor's answer came. He would not allow the tea ships to go.

Sam Adams stood up.

"This meeting," he said, "can do no more to save the country." It was a signal.

Outside a group of men dressed as Indians began yelling. They ran toward the harbor. Thousands of people from the meeting followed them. The "Indians," who were really the Sons of Liberty, rowed out to the tea ships. They tore open the boxes of tea and dumped all of it into the sea.

People jokingly called it "The Boston Tea-Party."

But it was a serious joke. The British were very angry. They said Sam Adams was "the chief of the Revolution" and they wanted to arrest him, put him in prison, and hang him. They said Boston must pay for the tea. The people refused. So the British closed Boston harbor. No ships could sail in or out.

There was much excitement all over America. Sam Adams said it was time for America to be free of Britain. He said America should no longer be a colony. It should be a free and independent country. All over America there was now talk of a meeting of men chosen by each colony. These men would get together in a big room. They would call themselves a "Congress" and they would talk about what to do.

In Massachusetts, Sam Adams was part of the House of Representatives. He wanted the House of Representatives to choose the men to go to the Congress.

But the governor had the power to send the representatives home if he did not like what they were doing. And if he found

they were choosing men to go to the Congress, he would surely do it. So at the meeting of the representatives Sam Adams wanted everyone to stay in the room until they had made their decision. "Don't let anyone in or out," he told the doorkeeper.

But one man who was a friend of the British pretended he was sick. The doorkeeper let him out and he rushed to the governor and told him what they were doing.

The governor quickly wrote an order saying that the representatives must end their meeting and go home. He gave the order to one of his men to read to the House of Representatives. The man hurried to the meeting hall, but the door was locked. And the doorkeeper could not let him in because he could not find the key. Sam Adams had taken the key and put it in his pocket.

The representatives finished choosing men to go to the Congress and then Sam unlocked the door.

Of course Sam Adams was chosen to go. And so was his younger cousin, lawyer John Adams, whom Sam had brought into Boston's struggle with the British. Later, John Hancock was chosen.

At the Congress most of the men wore fine clothes. But Sam Adams had on old clothes that his wife Betsy had sewed and patched and mended. He had no money to buy new clothes.

Too, Sam cared very little for money or things like clothes. When the general of the British army sent a messenger offering him money if he would stop making so much trouble for them, Sam told the messenger to leave and to tell the general he would never stop fighting for the rights of the people.

His friends in Boston wanted Sam to be dressed well when he went to the Congress. They thought that when he went to Philadelphia where the Congress was to meet it would not be right to have the leading man in America looking so shabby.

One evening there was a knock at his door and when he opened the door he saw a tailor who asked to measure him. Then a hatter came to the door and asked to measure his head. And a shoemaker came. None of them would say who had sent them or why.

A few days afterward a large trunk was left at the Adams house. In it was a suit, two pairs of shoes, a set of silver shoe buckles, gold knee buckles, a fine cocked hat, a gold-headed cane, and a red cloak.

It was a long bumpy carriage ride from Boston to Philadelphia, and Sam Adams's new clothes were wrinkled by the time he got there. Along the way people came out to meet the bold men from Massachusetts and invite them to dinner.

At the Congress the men from all over America talked about what to do. Sam Adams was known as the man who wanted America to be independent. And at first most men at the Congress did not agree. They were afraid of such a new and different idea. They had always been ruled by the king and Parliament. They thought they always would be. These men only wanted the king to be more fair. To leave the king would be like leaving home. They thought Sam Adams was a very dangerous man. Even John Adams did not yet think America should be free. Benjamin Franklin wanted America to have its rights but was still not sure about independence. George Washington believed in fighting back, but was strongly against making America an independent country.

Sam Adams tried to be calm but he was angry with the Congress. Independence was the only answer. It was that or surrender. He tried to be patient but when a friend wanted to know when the Congress would act on independence Sam said some in Congress made him think of "the tameness of the ox and the stupid servility of the ass." He knew one way that would change their minds. A demand from the people.

At this time a man named Thomas Paine wrote a little pamphlet called *Common Sense.* It said America should be free. It should not be ruled by a king. Tom Paine had grown up as a workingman, a mechanick. He reminded Sam of his boyhood friend, Bill. Tom Paine laughed at calling any man "sacred majesty." He said a king was only "a worm who in the midst of his splendor is crumbling into dust."

People all over America read Tom Paine's book. Some men

attacked it. But Sam Adams said it was right and most people said it was right. All over America people began to shout for independence.

Both Sam and his cousin John Adams spoke in Congress for independence. They argued. They persuaded. They demanded that Congress declare America free.

Finally as Britain continued to treat America badly and even to burn towns to punish the American people, even most of those with "the tameness of the ox and the stupid servility of the ass" came to agree that it was the only way.

At long last the Congress voted for independence. Then they wrote a paper called the Declaration of Independence. Young Thomas Jefferson from Virginia wrote most of it. It said that all people are created equal and they have equal rights that no one can take away.

That should be the happy end of the story, but it didn't really end that way.

A long war with Britain was fought and the American Army led by George Washington finally won. Sam Adams who had stayed in Philadelphia and been a leader in the war now went home to Boston and his wife, Betsy. America was now free.

Or was it?

Times were hard and some who had fought bravely in the Revolutionary War were now very poor. They did not have enough

money to pay their taxes. The government took their homes and put them up for sale to pay the money they owed.

And nobody helped them. Some people in Massachusetts got guns and tried to fight for their homes and their land. But soldiers came and drove them away. Even Sam Adams said the people were wrong. Perhaps it was because he was trying to make the new government work. Perhaps he was so worried about the new government that he forgot what it was like to have someone come to take your home away.

Sam Adams was no longer the leader of America. People called him "the Father of America" or "the Father of the American Revolution." And they were names he had earned. But he had now been pushed aside. A few wealthy men were gaining the power in America. He did not like it, but there was little he was able to do about it.

He explained the age-old problem in a letter to a friend:

"The haughty families think THEY must govern. The body of people tamely consent and submit to be their slaves." He added sadly, *"This unravels the mystery of millions being enslaved by the few. But my weak hand prevents my proceeding further."*

Still he kept on believing that some day the people would have the courage to end the rule of the few and rule themselves.